Riding the Comet

William Doreski

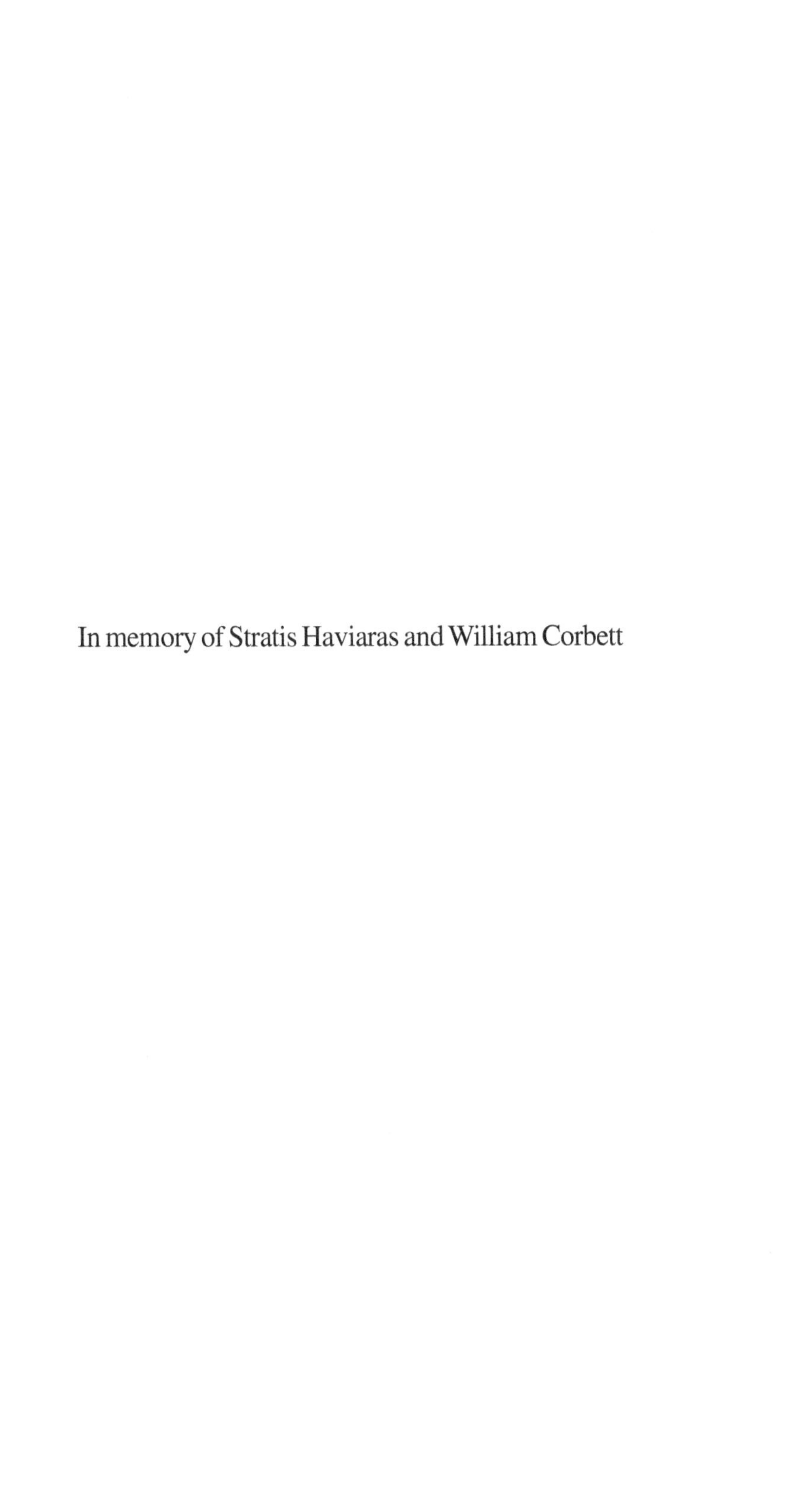

In memory of Stratis Haviaras and William Corbett

These poems have appeared in *The Academy of the Heart and Mind, Amsterdam Quarterly, As it Ought to Be, Avatar, Bangaluru Review, Barrow Street, Big Windows, Bleached Butterfly, Blue Five Notebook, Bombay Review, Cat / Prey, Chaos, Comstock Review, Constellate, Derail, Dissident Voices, Down in the Dirt, Euonia, 11 Mag Berlin, Flatbush Review, Flair, Frost Meadow Review, Global Polemic, Grand Little Things, Green Silk Journal, Gyroscope, Home Planet News, Ligeia, Listening Eye, London Grip New Poetry, Home Planet News, Metafore, Mineral Lit, Muddy River Poetry Review, Mycelium, Neon Garden, Night Picnic, Nine Muses, Pandemonium, Pacific Coast Journal, Paper Dragon, Pennsylvania English, Pensive, Poetica, Pocket Samovar, Rabid Oak, Raven Cage, Remington Review, River Oak Review, Sein und Werden, Smoky Quartz, Sobotka, Sparks of Calliope, Still Points Arts Quarterly, Stylus Lit, Thieving Magpie. Thimble, Third Wednesday, Tipton Poetry Journal, Tistelblomma, Two Thirds North, Unique, U-Rights Magazine, Vitni Review, West Trade, Westchester Review*. I am grateful to the editors of these journals.

Contents

Dark Passage

Toting a trapped mouse to the woods
at night, my headlamp burning.
When I open the trap the mouse
strolls out, pauses to paw smears
of peanut butter from its chops,
then ambles leisurely away.

The night is rolling big cigars
and smoking them fiendishly.
Stars pop like pimples. Gases
form nebulae larger than all
the life that has ever pulsated.

One fat little field mouse
embodies this energy as well
as the force of gravity does.
I'm glad I didn't kill it,
although its gritty life suggests
a casual lack of conscience.

The fan-shaped light I cast
as I walk back to the house
slashes through a deadweight of dark
that otherwise would oppress
and cause me to lose my bearings.

The ground underfoot retains
its illusion of solidity, but
trees have vaporized, leaving
only scars and stains on a wall.
I can't imagine a bat sailing
through this cast-iron dimension.

When I step into the breezeway,
a fully lit space, I snuff
the headlamp and become human
again, the hole I drilled in the dark
quickly healing behind me.

In the Present State of Witness

Strung out along the highway,
waving signs at grinning traffic,
our little clot of protest
suffers under judgmental sun.

Even in shade we wilt and nod
with a greedy vegetable thirst.
Local cops cruise us and wave
from air-conditioned vehicles

braced with massive bumpers
and armed with loaded shotguns.
You comment on every honk
and friendly gesture, count

the few rude middle fingers,
note that certain auto colors
seem friendlier than others.
Like kids on a boring road trip

we pass the hot noon hour
parsing tenor and baritone
registers of tooting horns.
The rare soprano or bass

confounds our calculations
but amuses and alerts us
to factors we can't account for.
So the protest protests itself

in the cool secret dark inside us.
The message of our signs exhorts
a more thoughtful and inclusive
lifestyle, urbane and sculpted

in the finest Carrara marble.
But America's too ramshackle
and nervous for such a vision,
the tattered pages of bibles

torn from tired old bindings
and wafting across rock-hard sky,
miming and mocking angel wings.
We'll never escape the politics

of barbecued meat suffering
as the thickest flavors must.
We'll never unravel every thread
of that fatuous Confederate flag

flying against a thunderstorm.
I watch you watching the traffic.
We look too small and irrelevant
to punctuate the national text.

But at least we hold our ground
more firmly than Charles the First
held England the moment before
his head fell into a basket.

The Last New England Elegy

We won't feel the same about ferns
bronzing in the October gloom.
We won't smell the burnt blue gossip
hazing above the village.
These modest deaths have wrung us dry
and left us fragile as wasp nests.

Vermont has become a monument,
while Maine has stuffed its pockets
with stones and stepped into the sea.
New Hampshire's flannel shirt has torn,
Rhode Island has paved itself flat.
Connecticut no longer cares,
Massachusetts repents in sighs.

You read the map from south to north
while I scan it west to east.
We will never feel the same
about the snarls of numbered routes,
about the folds and tears and stains
and the mapmaker's famous colors.

These little deaths have severed
interstate highways and stranded
motorists who were driving drunk
with all their zippers undone.
The grief has sickened the maples,
which will fail to bud in April
when only flowerings count.

Can the outer planets console us?
Tonight they'll shrug right up to us
and lave us in toxic ammonias
as we sleep off the steepest angles.
What's left? Our surviving pets
mutter in their private language
as the good garden soil turns over
and over, restless and gnostic
as it sorts its worms and grubs.

Thanks to Jonathan Edwards

Black spiders in my woodpile
asterisk a sharp distinction
between their brisk compaction
and the expansive human view.
These spiders aren't the toxic
species that gleam in cellars
or crawl into children's bunk beds.
They're only shy little blobs
dedicated to devouring gnats.

Splitting oak and maple to burn
on spangled winter nights, I brush
these tiny creatures to safety
without damaging their many
but necessary legs. The image
of a spider in a candle flame,
thanks to Jonathan Edwards,
has cursed literate New England
for almost three hundred years.

I'd like to spider myself off
to fresh quarters, new horizons,
more limber self-expressions.
If I could do it by compressing
myself into an iota
of punctuation I surely would.
But my hulking muddle of flesh
has committed itself to culture
rather than nature, shriving itself

of several vital dimensions
that neither ink on paper
nor the digital screen can display.

The rumble of the gas engine,
the sheer of splitting firewood,
the muscle of piling the product
belong to the great world of work
that every creature inhabits.
But my daydreams of spiderhood
empowered by simple purpose
lilt into the stratosphere
like so many runaway blimps.

Freewheeling

Bicycling downstream on back roads
from Walpole to Keene I feel
as supple as well-worn suede.
With grave ancient empathy
the brown hills flex in the breeze.
Brooks twinkle in gutters of stones.
The roads pour down through valleys
scraped by glaciers, smoothed by age
to resemble flesh folded on flesh
after acts of bristling love.

I remember everything: turtles
basking in the emerald marsh,
herons lancing the ooze for newts,
minnows shivering like chain mail.
That was the moment I became
the self that bicycles downhill
at terrible speed, lathering
shadows that surf across landscapes
with reckless but actual purpose.

I haven't plied that marsh in decades.
But as I flash past wooden houses
that withhold their grim expressions
I free myself from scalded cities
and silt-encrusted suburbs
of the adulthood I've never earned,
and let a single note fly.

No one hears me or cares if
I crash into a friendly boulder
dumped from an ice sheet ages
before I fully evolved. Knit
and purl of the last bird call
caresses the flight I've taken
from one lost town to another—
the roads left clutching their scripts
and the small uncharted places
fulfilled for one sunny moment
while treefrogs gather their breath.

Shave, Sheer, Slick

Shaving pleases me. The soap
and lather, the polished blade,
the stroke, the varied textures
of skin exposed to sharpness.
All the *s* sounds: shave, sheer, slick.

This morning I shear four days
of weed from my homely façade.
The razor slides across my flesh
like a toboggan over snow.
I rinse the razor and basin

and look hard into the mirror
as if reading Plato in Greek.
I know nothing of his language
beyond the alphabet and half
a hundred words and phrases.

I know nothing of this person
reflected tooth and pore but
his gnash and grind of being.
To my left, through the window,
the landscape I tend with mower,

loppers, pruning saw regards me
with an earthy resentment only
the vegetable world can indulge.
Everything is about cut and trim.
Less is more. Fashion requires

women to bare themselves almost
discreetly, black gowns cut to show
whatever men shouldn't look at,
swimsuits far more aggressive
than actual point-blank nudity.

In teaching writing, we agree
that cutting a text is preferable
to elongation. So why not
leave the page as blank as skin
after the usual morning shave?

Less is more, but not with money.
Counting a pocketful of change
to buy a few stamps to mail
letters I shouldn't have written,
or unrolling a greasy wad

of one-dollar bills to pay
the grocery store clerk staring
at my shaven but rumpled mug
shames me as much as the rust
spangling my old Toyota.

Maybe in the next life I'll grow
a luxurious mink of a beard.
No one will believe it's me,
the feel of it suave and silken,
the grace of it stirred by the wind.

Drowning Aloud

New clothes and a summer tan
fail to impress you. I try,
but the whirlpools of your eyes

draw people like me below
the surface, where we flail
with fear of drowning aloud.

So many cries for help, so few
efforts to rescue us. You laugh
away my terror, and critique

my latest outfit: duck-green
trousers with a nerd-blue shirt.
At least my shoes escape notice.

Wagging dogs walking past
observe me with curious snouts
as they scout for delicate odors.

Their owners look away although
their clothes are as casual as mine.
Maybe my sunburn violates

the ethnic and racial concepts
we learned to label in school.
You don't care how tawny or brazen

my clothes, skin, or expression.
You like to hear me struggling
in perfectly breathable air.

Lately your political stance
has toughened with layers of asphalt.
I would never challenge a word

of your one-person party line.
But going under for the third
and final time I invoke

your candidate, whose graze
almost exceeds yours in depth,
his big ripe hands all over you,

his leer a slash of crimson.
When the rest of us finish
drowning aloud you'll savor

the utter silence that follows,
your future nailed to a tree
where any survivor can read it.

Yellow Morning Sky

A plain yellow morning sky
nails itself to my forehead.
You complain that I don't watch
enough old movies to brace myself
against the crush of daily news.
Keaton, Chaplin, Lloyd. Agreed,
these ossified figures should,
in real-world conditions, sate me
with humor enough to survive
the windiest political angst.

But I can't focus long enough
on small-screen imagery plaited
in bits and bytes in shades of gray
that remind me of virus swarming
under electron microscopes.
You promised an improved life
unsheathed by digital forces,
but reduced yourself to a self
captured by Zoom and pointed
my way like a weapon of war.

I'm more alone than ever,
the crystal voices stilled at last.
A fresh wind moves the trees
with large but neutral gestures.
The sky stuck to my forehead
flaps like a sheet of paper.
Remember when we named things

after their ordinary function?
Paper, pencil, hammer, wrench?

The old movies flow through the ether
with Mary Pickford smiling
and the Gish sisters distraught.
They've lingered too long and hardened
like paint. I'd like to revive them
on a screen as big as the sky,
but that sickly yellow tint
renders everyone foolish and wan.

Arrested for Decay

Today I've arrested myself for decay. Yes, I know that Jack Kerouac was also charged with that disorder. But his came about through hard drinking, which I couldn't sustain. My decay is more private than my liver and pancreas. It seats itself in a gland that scientists haven't yet discovered. Maybe not everyone bears this gland. I don't know. A railroad bridge over a swirl of river. A freight train slashes across the bridge. This is a unit train, a mile of shipping containers pulled by a pair of six-thousand horsepower diesels. I inhale their rich exhaust, ripened by effort. Despite its tremendous weight, this train must be going seventy miles an hour. With a little foresight I could have caught it in the yard, crawled into one of the containers after respectfully breaking the seal. But I missed my opportunity and must remain here in a state of decay that reeks like an abandoned sewage plant. That's the gland, you see. It makes itself known. As I start walking toward our village jail, the train disappears into the folded landscape.

The Present Tense Lacks Genius

If this modest river is different
every time I see it, why not
build a dam and cure its rage
to continually reform itself?

Even under a skim of ice,
its righteous flow asserts itself
and shames my gradual slippage
through the interstices of age.

You rarely hear me speak aloud
anymore, but read my thoughts
the way I read the black current
fulfilling the angst of gravity.

In the café with certain friends
beaming around us you ply
your conversational prowess
in the richest possible flow

while I slip into my coffee
to drown a lifetime of being shy.
The present tense lacks genius,
lacks a foothold on the slope

that has steepened since my birth.
When I look into the shallows
flowing through absolute cold
or hear you parsing politics

with a surgeon's bristling word-hoard,
I feel slight enough to bookmark,
with a child's absolute certainty,
a moment in a roughhewn life.

Tomorrow I'll forget this urge
to pin myself to a paper chart
and dangle like a pelt. For now,
though, the dark waters flow and flow,

and so does your conversation,
which no more than the river
would accept my intervention,
not even with a brittle smile.

The Ruins of Knossos

(in memory of Jack Gilbert)

You knelt in the ruins of Knossos
and prayed for your broken life.
Something answered, showering you
with elegiac rage. The window
of the palace overlooked the sea,

but distantly, a line etched
on a cloudy-bright horizon.
Although you rejected flimsy
and inconsequential writing,
so much San Francisco remained

you could hardly remember Pittsburgh,
where the mythical rivers meet,
site of your most eloquent disdain.
Maybe Crete and the smaller islands
also lingered beyond their use.

Maybe your lover, dead of cancer,
flowered like a prologue rather
than flail in violet shadows.
No one can say, since your death
has canceled your dementia.

Maybe you've returned to work
in steel. Maybe your degree
has finally taken root

and grounded you inside yourself,
where there isn't a sea-view

anymore. The islands drift
on the edge of the known world.
The modest skyscrapers of Pittsburgh
punctuate the unknown world
and skewer your heart. The fuzz

of beard you sported at last
framed you in the palest light
to commemorate the distance
between Knossos and the heavens
you tried so hard to endorse

Reading About Ophelia

Reading about Ophelia,
I worry that her useless pallor
has condemned her to Hamlet's disdain.

Yet Hamlet's nowhere in sight.
Ophelia's mooning over nothing,
the wind sweeping down from Norway

to rifle her ropy yellow hair.
Some Freudian commentators
insist that Polonius took

her virginity in her childhood,
leaving her useless to Hamlet
and his adolescent perversions.

Some say that drawn to water
and mayflowers she regressed
to self-dissolution in nature.

Still others claim that her brother
and lover left her adrift
and pregnant while Hamlet slept

so dreamily with his mother
he hardly noticed his uncle's
mild and befuddled reproach.

I'll read until she drowns herself
and then I'll mourn her as thoroughly
as anyone does; her child's heart stilled

and the cold wind from Norway
blowing for dozens of centuries
around and around the world.

Res Luto Materia

On mud flats we find a growth
we've never seen, sponge-like
with six-inch pores. The pulp of it
feels like the brown upholstery
of a car from the 1940s.
The opaque mass of this matter
covers a thousand square feet
and crests over ten feet tall.
You insist that we destroy it
before it slumps over the rest
of the shoreline, devolving
into the grossest appetite.
But only in a horror film
of the Fifties could lumps like this
animate and slop into the world,
devouring whatever they touch.
This blot of fungus will squelch
when the next spring tide occurs.
Feel it: cold as a side of beef.
Peer into the big pores and see
only the simplest kind of dark.
Yes, I can feel the faintest throb
of life, a dim sensibility
wrestling itself into shape.
Still, it's only a fungal mind
groping for a host, unable
to perceive or appreciate
the red-streaked dusk, the wet mud
shining like a coat of mail.

Let's return to solid ground
and get fish and chips and beer
at the little restaurant just opened
for the season. Let this creature—
animal, vegetable, mineral—
simmer in the simple perfection
that more self-conscious beings
mistake for lack of ambition.

Revenge of the Dryads

Wood nymphs return after years
of misogynistic religion
to reclaim their natural fibers.

You spot and photograph one
preening in the autumn glare.
Her posture embodies a strength

I envy for its flexible stance.
I've always wanted to meet
a dryad gleaming in shade

on an August afternoon so pale
the landscape loses all color
and all but the one dimension.

But to see one striding naked
through autumn chill would shiver me
to the bone, exposing my ego

to her curious balsamic gaze.
I'm glad you took this photo
and returned from the forest

with your mind more or less intact.
Although they love real heroes
they can get grumpy when seen

by ordinary flesh-bags like us.
I wish I could write an epic
starring both of us and pin it

page by page to favorite trees.
The dryads go unclothed except
for bark and fiber. They eat

little snacks dropped from heaven,
which for them is in the tree-tops.
You would enjoy that life,

but being a carbon-based creature
can't join their textual splendor.
If I were a satyr I'd dash

headlong into the woods to cavort;
but I'm only a limp old fellow
who has read too many books

and has seen too many photos
that have stolen too many souls
and left delusions in their wake.

Atop the Acropolis

Swimming uphill through the heat
to the lip of the Acropolis,
I touch every cut and broken stone
as if comforting the dead
of a hundred pointless wars.

The square temple of Athena
with its eager caryatids
greets me with a toothy grin.
I should have brought a bottle
of cold and potable water,

but hadn't realized the ascent
would feel desperate as my attempt
to learn to read ancient Greek
in a couple of summer months.
The city lounging below this height

hides in whatever shade it can find.
Along Athens' squared-off avenues,
limestone blocks taper in distance
fizzy with an Aegean mist.
A hundred cafes offer chairs

sturdy enough for the tourists
who've tired of the crumbled wrecks
of a culture they can't pronounce.
I turn to face the last few steps
with the noon sun pounding me flat.

What's left of the Parthenon,
roofless and bluff with scaffolding,
combs the humid air with columns
of such Doric purity I'd kiss them
if the smirking guards allowed.

A construction crane in the midst
of the wreckage the Turks left
in the seventeenth century
seems poised to prey on anyone
braving that ghostly interior.

An avid crowd shrugs me aside
in its rush to snap the famous
ruin that only the mating
of art, geology and faith
in a reckless moment explains.

Volterra

In Volterra the many churches scrub themselves clean in the case-hardened sun. Chiesa di San Giusto Nuovo with its yellow interior cheerful as a kindergarten; The Cattedrale do Santa Maria Assunta creaky with scaffolding spiderwebbing the apse and choir, its blue and white arches looking nervous but aloof; Chiesa di Sant' Andrea with its attached seminary brooding. You worry about the altar boys trapped in these compressed hill villages. The air pressure is conducive to lechery, while the ancient stonework is too rigid to stoop to notice the shy little faces looking up at the godless blue. Near the Etruscan museum, on Via Don Giovanni Minzoni, we pause for coffee almost too rich and black to drink. The streets are nearly too narrow for my shoulders. I don't understand the red and white flags everywhere. The flag of Tuscany? The flag of successful seduction? No, don't ask the waiter. We're alien to all local concepts, and the towel on his arm is spotless. Besides, the long shadows creeping down the street will soon engulf us in gray. Once we're part of the scenery, we'll understand that the flags are fluttering in memory of us and the Etruscans, from whom so much has evolved.

That Mussolini Grimace

Letter bombs arrive almost daily,
bursting with impotent bluster.
Killer drones crash in the trees.
Drunks toss their trash in our driveway
and speed away howling with rage.

We should never have spoken up
when authoritarian gestures
came into fashion, that stern
Mussolini grimace deployed
among the rural population.

Now I patrol our boundaries
with a killer cat straining
at the leash. Now and then
dead snipers occur in the brush,
their rifles rusted, their bones

flensed by congeries of mice.
I'm sure they died of boredom,
having oversold themselves
on the glamor of their profession.
You've noted the occasional

dirigible drifting overhead,
but I haven't seen one since
the war with Canada ended.
The people at the post office
sort the letter bombs from other

worst-class mail and bag them
in steel mesh to muffle the blast.
Simple drones can't penetrate
the forest canopy that shields
our house from airborne assault.

We resolve never to speak aloud
again, the Mussolini grimace
 splashed across *Vogue* and *Elle*,
killer instincts aestheticized
in colors too dull to run.

Self-Storage

These long and narrow boxes
contain the rolled-up spirits
of people we've tried to love.

Some died in metal on metal.
Some ballooned and exploded.
Some drifted far out to sea.

Some haven't died yet but shed
their ghosts when they lost their faith
in the scent and texture of things.

We tried so hard, but our smiles
crumpled like melons gone bad
and collapsed with shy apologies.

How can we atone for a lack
of sin that in some circumstance
might have staved off boredom?

What should we do with these boxes?
Dozens of them, wood or cardboard
or quality high-test vinyl?

We could rent a self-storage unit
and justify the expense
with all the selves we have to store.

But what if some spirits ooze
from their boxes, unroll
and reshape themselves to haunt?

What if other people renting
space for old furniture and books
complain of the groans and sighs?

Let's stack the boxes downstairs
and hope that if the basement floods
the spirits quietly drown.

But maybe they'd just get moldy
and smell of rank archaeologies
we're too amateur to perform.

Down Holt Road

A narrow strip of asphalt
hemmed by the season's new leaves.
"Dead End" doesn't describe it.
A break in the trees exposes
a neatly graveled paddock

with a wide view down the slope.
I've never seen a horse prancing
in this manicured place, but often
pause to admire the panorama
featuring Grand Monadnock framed

by the open, white-enameled gate.
The way this lonely spot maintains
this expensive view impresses me
with a grasp of bold abstraction
only a painter as brilliant,

drunk, and crazy as Jackson Pollock
could capture and hang on a wall.
I wish I didn't love clarity
and could render this perspective
in a slew of unlikely angles,

working language like a blowtorch.
What if I lie in the gravel long enough
for a ghost horse to trample me?
Would I have to suffer my injuries
all night until dawn refreshed

the scene in slightly altered colors?
Then would I rise completely healed
and walk home with confidence
I haven't felt in a lifetime?
A couple of warblers chirp

in the foliage to my left.
A flicker of white fur reveals
a deer in the trees to the right.
Straight ahead the mountain slumps
in its deeply weathered posture.

It has haunted me all my life;
but in this carefully framed moment
it embodies the form and content
I sought in flesh and intellect
but never fully possessed.

Alligators in New Hampshire

Alligators have colonized our marsh. Climate change has rendered New Hampshire so warm that these creatures have migrated by the dozens, toting their human-hide luggage. They cackle, whisper, and snarl as they sample the mud and slither about in search of food. I walk down to the edge of the marsh to watch them. One friendly fellow sidles up with a big smile. His teeth look like scrimshaw. His breath reeks of some raw creature. His tough hide flatters him. His rubbery muscular torso looks powerful as a turbine. I speak to him in simple sentences most local reptiles and amphibians understand. He nods with a hint of wisdom and opens and shuts his jaws as if fumbling for words. I don't expect an actual response, of course, but the glimmer in his eyes is unmistakable. We gaze at each other in a friendly way for a while. The warm smell of the marsh thickens with gnats and flies. Then he turns, dragging his limber tail, and slumps back into the shallows. I look over the sullen expanse and note the eyes watching me in the summer dusk. The oily water looks like broth. Hundreds of frogs had been croaking here since the thaw, but now I don't hear a one.

October Drift

After jamming a finger
in the gas-powered wood splitter,
I express myself in blue and orange

that complements the autumn glare.
You listen with the tuned ear
of an acoustic folk music fan,

but hardly pause in your work.
The crimp of my finger means
nothing like the snap of twigs

as deer browse on the far edge
of the garden, brown against brown.
I yanked it free before it broke—

before prose imagination
severed the day from its image.
The bruise and modest rip

of flesh will heal so quickly
the deer will never suspect me
of sharing their slim mortality.

You're raking the local leaves
with such fervor that your aspect
ratio is constantly shifting.

A narrow glance, then a broad one,
then back to narrow as you scan
the rubble for black-legged ticks,

pinpricks of chronic disease.
I continue feeding chunk after chunk
of log to the grumbling machine.

My little offering of pain
doesn't impress the universe.
Neither does your raking startle

the last oak leaves to free themselves
and fall obliging at your feet.
Maybe we should stop looking

for shape and design and start
all over again with a cosmos
too clumsy to acknowledge a plan.

The breeze picks up. Leaves skitter
across the driveway. The splitter
coughs itself out of gas. Silence

startles us both, and we look up
by instinct to see the clouds fly,
the afternoon light depleted.

Seven-Sided Curse

You read in a book that seven
sided objects, landscapes, people
offend nature, flesh, and spirit.

Your new distrust of heptagons
infects your daily perceptions.
With a tidbit of clever math

you prove that my rectangular
desk has three invisible sides
and has secretly undermined me

for at least the last twenty years.
You also demonstrate that walking
to the brook to watch it trill

over rocks and form black pools
shapes a seven-sided argument
against faith in human progress.

I should stay home and read books
on the simple calculus of form.
High-school plane geometry

wasn't enough to prepare me
for the asymmetries of the world.
Heptagons are both regular

and not. I used to admire them,
but you claim they brainwashed me
in puberty when a young woman

offered seven sides of herself
without revealing anything
but moonlight the color of bone.

You know me better than history;
so when you warn me against
further consorting with heptagons

I promise that while admiring
winter constellations I'll count
only even numbers of stars.

Black and White and Gray All Over

Down a steep muddy driveway,
the auto restorer's garage.
A character in a film noir,
I'll drive the '53 Hudson
to a notorious crime scene,
 then abandon it with a body
bent and stinking in the trunk.

You don't believe this will happen,
but this plot is destined for film stock
left over from my childhood
when big men shaped like bullets
warped women with their dialogue—
a mélange of flattery and tough.

Look, this driveway is real enough
to muddy my shoes. The car
with its low windshield gleaming
in sloping afternoon sunlight
has already conveyed a corpse
or two in its long slow career.

Listen to that big engine throb,
spewing enough hydrocarbons
to fatally tilt the climate
in the course of one long road trip
from the east coast to the west,
from obscurity to stardom.

The restorer is a grimy fellow
who plays many casual roles
in his own life and others'.
Didn't you have an affair with him
a year or two before your birth?
As I drive away, he returns
to the shadows and folds like a bat.

At the top of the driveway you stand
with folded arms, rebuking me
for adopting this alternative life—
so grainy and underexposed
we hardly recognize each other
except as exigent forms.

Odes to Satan

Witches' Sabbath comes around
again, bears at the bird feeder,
rain drooling from the eaves.

You wanted a decent silence
to roll over and flatten the land,
refreshing us with wildflowers,

which ghosts of the fallen tribes
acknowledge in their language
and value for medicinal use.

We could use some good medicine
now that the plague is churning
in cities gone gray with distance,

as Dickinson seemed to predict.
The few surviving witches
are a surly lot, their magic

abused by politicians eager
for re-election, misused
by economists bent on proving

that wealth deserves its cache.
You hope the rain clears by dark
so we can join the witches

romping around their barbecue
in the heart of the heart of forest.
I'd rather stay home and watch

TV shows from my childhood,
when everything was black and white.
I'd rather drink ginger tea and nod

with mortal sleep than listen
to gnarled figures chanting
their trite little odes to Satan,

who has done his work on earth
and left us gazing into mirrors
to study our wrinkled grins.

The day decants in weather
the color of last winter's socks.
Hyacinth and daffodils smirk.

Maybe there won't be a sabbath
celebrated in the woods behind
our house. Maybe the loggers

felled too many trees, allowing
sun and moonlight to sterilize
the mossy places of sacrifice

where night-vapors fostered dreams
that innocent people like us
mistook for our daily lives.

The Gospel of the Mist

In my dream I devise a mist
that if breathed for one whole day
cures even the rudest cancer.
Celebrities flock to inhale it.
Poor folks stand in line for hours.
Local politicians endorse it.
The most famous cancers shrivel
into pellets the body excretes.
The more subtle tumors regress
with tiny cries of dismay
and die of their disappointment.

The mist doesn't smell or taste
medicinal. It's a tang of pine
mingled with an effervescence
of orange sherbet and bourbon.
Even people without cancer
like bathing in the spa I've built
to house my miracle cure.
It's only a shack I constructed
of lumber from the local landfill,
but it keeps rain from diluting
the mist and chilling the patients.

Although this cure makes me famous,
I worry that the side effects
of inhaling such a pleasant taste
will leave people dissatisfied
with their fragile little lives

and encourage public suicide
with colorful methods and modes.
Still, I collect my modest fees
and hope that the miracle lasts,
the taste of the mist so gentle
it lingers like a French kiss
impressed by a wanton child.

A Paper Lightning Bolt

Someone has tacked a paper cutout
of a lightning bolt to the sky.
One of those zigzag cartoons
that Thor likes to chuck at the earth.

No, it doesn't look like real lightning,
but I wonder how the cartoonist
got it up there, how it's fastened
to the filmy and fickle sky.

You think it fell from a comet
and somehow stuck into place
through an obscure natural process
science has yet to describe.

But looking through binoculars
I can clearly see that it's paper
rippling in a stratospheric wind.
We agree it's not an omen but

perhaps a campaign poster
for a candidate running for
some minor public office
like fence viewer or dog warden.

Other people are looking up.
A woman panics, fears the hand
of God is working against us.
But God doesn't bother with paper

silhouettes when he can wield
the real thing with deadly effect.
We sip our latte outdoors because
the pandemic still prevails.

The first good thunderstorm
will pulp that phony lightning bolt
in a gust of cosmic laughter
we'll hear even if asleep.

No one should be worried,
but I wonder who owns a ladder
tall enough to reach all that sky
and whether he'd lend it to me.

Green Auroras

In the news, we learn that Israel
has failed to form a government,
that our President still refuses
to feel impeached. Thin blue snow
decorates the back yard at dawn.
Should we be combing the distance
for clues to our spiritual past?
Or should we be reading tea leaves
to generate future protocols?

We're small people cemented
into small lives in a small town
that used to be "arty" but embraced
real estate as its destiny.
Should we drape ourselves in cabbage
and pretend we're harvest figures
from the early Renaissance?
Should we become pumpkin-headed
to acknowledge American values?

The pages are still dark despite
the burnishing of the early sky.
Even if turned by our breath
they would tell us nothing new,
nothing we could frame and hang
where local art used to hang.
If we stepped outdoor to orate
with a single voice, the climate
would shift an inch or two and blame us

for being the very fossil fuel
that shames the naked atmosphere.

We should hunker over ourselves
and be glad of a few last days
and the green auroras that lately
have been mocking the otherwise
colorless nights that deny us
the depth we would like to deploy.

The Difference Between Subject and Object

Certain objects dislike me.
My digital camera cringes
and tucks its tiny controls
whenever I fondle it.
My car develops a cough
if I attempt to drive it more
than a couple of miles to the store.
A pot clatters and smashes
a drinking glass in the dishpan.
The clock looks at me in horror.
The washer gnashes my clothes to rags.

Maybe it's not only me but all
flesh that incites rebellion
in objects tired of being objects.
Does the inanimate always war
against organic evolution,
sparking that infinite high note
that sometimes tingles my hearing?
I suspect an unscientific
overlap between this world
and a parallel one occurs
when the moon strikes a certain pose
to remind everyone that
it's sometimes wise to go naked.

Breaking down the difference
between subject and object requires
grammatical and material

bravado; but mechanical
and digital devices, cast iron
and plastic already express
more courage and persistence than me.
I wish I could recover some
of the human ingenuity
that endowed things with such spirit.

The simpler inorganics, rocks
and standing or flowing water,
don't even notice, let alone
trouble me the way manufactured
objects in their wisdom do.
Picking broken glass from the dishpan,
I cut myself. As the blood spreads
in the sudsy water the pot smiles
a dark old smile, and the clock ticks
with a chuckle that make me laugh.

Not Ourselves, and Others

In the Metropole Hotel
our room replays the whispers
of lovers dead a hundred years.
The man whispers in your ear,
the woman whispers in my ear.
They mistake us for ourselves
and propose to seduce us
in bravura ecstasy no one
but astronomers tracking comets
or dancers in mid-leap enjoy.

But we're not ourselves. The flight
to Berlin passed through ether
replete with uncanny spirits
that displaced our own. Landing,
we realized that someone else
combed our hair, washed our hands, flushed
the sanitary airport toilets.
We looked in mirrors and saw
a gray mist where our faces
had been when we left Heathrow.

The eye believes its lies so
we became no one particular,
generalized beyond recognition.
When we checked in, we both signed
the register in gray ink that faded
before the desk clerk could read it.
I don't know whose names we used,

but our credit cards still apply
and our luggage still looks familiar.

Now the whispers blunt themselves
against our utter lack of fact.
The oily persuasions would work
if we could confide in these bodies,
which may or may not be ours.
We could still indulge ourselves
and them, plying certain organs
we may have retained from our past
and from everyone else's past.

But what if the war returns
and the bombs flash and bluster
and gusty speeches soil the night
with bravado sex can't appease?
We lie in the skins of strangers
and allow the alien whispers
to buffet our lingering senses
with a promise of communion
the feeble lamplight and frozen
night at the window oppose.

The Void Has Never Healed

On Bleeker Street a moment
of declension as we realize
how dark and alone we are.

In this age of quarantine
the city has clenched a fist,
but keeps its rage to itself.

The buses have stopped running.
Grates bar the subway entries.
Cabstands are holes in a void.

Even trash cans have withdrawn
to sulk in basements or alleys.
With everyone out of business

the hulks of retail space loom
with the angst of ancient Egypt.
If only rain would prattle

on the still black asphalt we'd feel
lively enough to rush along
to brighter and bolder spaces.

But the void has never healed.
The page hasn't turned for years
despite the basking of skyscrapers

girdled about Midtown, the greed
of museums to reclaim the past.
We could fall in step with the dead

cluttering the basement morgues
of hospitals all over town.
Or we could huddle in this doorway

until a creamy sunrise shucks
the creepy old shrouds to expose
the tender parts of Manhattan

where accumulation for its own sake
continues like the patter of mice
through rooms too dusty to rent.

Mask Upon Mask

To don surgical masks means
layering mask upon mask,
concealing what's always concealed.
The fresh new disposable mask—
simple, disfiguring, blunt—
covers the permanent one—
complex, form-fitting, sly,
permeable to every slight.

Everyone is sporting these:
trapping their moist breath to foster
mildew the color of bruises.
Our coughs and sneezes occur
only in the dark. The virus
that has sculpted our routines
seeps through every precaution,
its innocence so evolved
it can kill without regret.

Still, we render fashionable
whatever we can't avoid.
Some people sport paisley masks,
some checked, some embroidered
with messages too small to read
at a safe impersonal distance.
We stick to plain disposables
in white or that depressing blue
seen only in clinical settings.

Even walking in the woods,
we meet fellow masks struggling
to keep from touching their faces.
Our muffled hellos resound
in organs we hadn't plumbed before.
Soon we'll riot behind our masks,
running amok inside ourselves,
everyone sick of being good—
being good enough to survive.

Everyone Seen in Profile

Do you believe that the heft
of our village keeps us happy?

Excess weight flattens landscapes
and ruins laws of perspective.

Our former police chief pushes
a belly as blunt as Moby-Dick.

A neighbor's car squeals in its springs
as she plumps into the driver's seat.

We're so bored with ourselves we eat
objects of clashing colors

as if nutrition weren't the issue.
How long will drought and disease

edge us into private places
where it's hard to cast a shadow?

Why don't the thin men of Haddam
respond to our bleating and sighs?

When winter arrives, we'll stand around
drinking coffee in snowdrifts.

Unsafe to step indoors where
viral thoughts linger long after

the subject has become a verb.
For now, the autumn wind teases

with a moveable sterile field
in which we enjoy our morning snack.

Eventually the town will collapse
under the excess of its populace.

The river, astringent with drought,
will equivocate for awhile

but eventually flush away the fat
and leave the bones posed in dance

to tease some later generation
with scenes to paint on cave walls—

as if we could be disciplined
to live modestly in caves.

Your Green Shadow

Sleet hisses on the roofs of Keene.
My umbrella is a bat wing
angled for flight. Epitaphs

mourn the thick air exuding
from sports bars and bagel shops.
Your faith in astrology shapes

your footfall from one occasion
to the next. Walking beside me,
beyond me, you incite a green

shadow cast by the lamplight,
defying the colorless weather.
How can I recite the last canto

of *Paradiso*, invoking
egos snuffed centuries ago
in art we admire but resist?

How can I resurrect someone
who died young inside you only
to rebirth herself in thousands

of tiny ghosts swarming like flies?
You laugh because I'm oblique
as the sleet fizzing underfoot.

You laugh when your green shadow
trips me and I sprawl in the wet,
my bones creaking but unbroken,

my umbrella bent beneath me
like a bit of punctuation
misplaced in the midst of a phrase.

The Peruvian Language

The planet has over-ripened,
and threatens to burst and spill
geologic seed in the vacuum.

The blush of unrequited day
fulfills my dream of learning
some lost Peruvian language,

a language of pointed mountains
and civilizations trampled
by hard little men sweating

in armor far too big for them.
I don't refer to Aymara
or Quechua but rather speech

without sound, a silent homage
to heights and depths unsoiled by maps,
and lakes and salt flats and even

modern cities casting shadows
that sink into stone to linger.
I want to learn this unknown language

before I catch a plane to Lima,
where a mob will overthrow me
before I speak a single word.

Later, walking slowly and even
more slowly up the stilted trail
to Machu Picchu, I'll hear

ghostly whispers that don't exist
but which carry grave abstractions
vital to my mental hygiene.

Still later, in a Cusco sidewalk
café, I'll eavesdrop on people
perplexed by each other's syntax.

Toughened by mountain exercise,
I'll be able to parse the real
Peruvian from the excess.

When I return to the hotel,
I'll be dragging an authentic
shadow tough enough to anchor me

to some portion of the planet
that will survive the explosion
and enjoy the laugh that follows.

Conspiring with Entropy

Forest isn't synonymous
with *wood*, since English
forests don't have to have trees.
Does that offend you? Beware
of Old French, the source not only
of etymologies but rank
or rancorous confusion, not
compatible with contusions.

After two days of snow and ice
the landscape looks too gray and bruised
to answer the simplest questions.
Before the forest—defined as
wild land set aside for hunting—
moves any closer, flexing its boughs,
we must scrape away driveway ice
so we can move about freely
with candor and lack of want.

We can't let the *forestam silvam*
hem us in. Too much Latin
can choke an adult or a child
lacking a good dictionary.
Yesterday watching the snow flop
from the roof I thought I detected
irony in simple gravity,
a conspiracy with entropy.

All those *y* sounds mating without
a sprig of phonetic conscience.
As if reading Muldoon's poetry
could stopper the oncoming moment
when everything goes blank forever
and you lean over the coffin and sigh
or laugh or look stoic as a sheep.

The forest, more precisely woodland
with seasonal hunting allowed,
shrugs off the bone-warping cold
and waves at the creamy sunlight
as if soliciting a bribe.

Cosmic Overture

A cold Thanksgiving. The forest
creaks like a haunted hotel.
Yesterday's tire tracks fossilize.
The crimes for which I'd hoped
to be remembered snuff out
in snow drifts callous as egos.
In the adamantine daylight
the planets swirl into view.

Mercury shivery with heat,
Venus shrouded in aqua mist.
Mars a flammable bull's-eye,
Saturn ringed and ringed and ringed.
Jupiter with its huge open eye.
Uranus so foully misnamed,
Neptune waving a cosmic trident.
Pluto limping through its wide, wide arc.
I can even see Earth brimming
in the wrong end of a telescope.
Didn't Holst write *The Planets*
to prepare me for this holiday?

No big dinner for me. Years
of power outages and lack
of immediate family suggest
a modest and thrifty approach
to this post-imperial moment.
Two dozen wild turkeys ransack
bird feeders intended for juncos,

chickadees, titmice, purple finch.
A couple of handfuls of corn
distract the big birds but draw
whitetails from the groaning woods.

The planets whirl in gaudy orbits
like carnival rides overhead.
The turkeys don't seem to notice,
the deer browse without spooking;
but I fear that the solar system
has downscaled to fit itself
into my faulty little vision—
the cold bright sky now lacking
some necessary dimension
that used to keep the distance at bay.

Parisian War Song

Felling white pine saplings
is nearly as crude as surgery.
The bite of the pruning saw
or the gnawing of loppers

opens wounds beyond healing.
I pity these uprights toppled
many decades before their prime.
Too much like the infantry

marched into enemy fire
to satisfy those generals
who count success in lives lost
rather than in the ground gained.

Before I gathered my tools,
I reread Rimbaud's "Parisian
War Song," a ditty suitable
for this fouled and murky spring.

Do I care who Thiers and Picard
were? The first was president
of the Republic, the other
would have surrendered to Prussia

after the Battle of Sedan.
I would never have surrendered
to Prussia or any other
defunct kingdom unless

Walt Disney had crowned the king.
The rest of Rimbaud's poem
not only nods over history
but snores aloud. Still, the blood-stained

waters rise over the globe,
and the peasants in the bushes
will have less cover when I've trimmed
these saplings to open the view.

Patrolling the Border

The sun rises, looks around,
withdraws to regain its courage.
Up again, it still looks timid
as a tulip. I'm out early,
plucking trash from the roadside,
hoping to encourage bunchberry,
clintonia, and wild ginger—
flowers gone nearly extinct
after flourishing for decades
along our dead-end road. The day
promises and promises but
won't follow through. Orpheus
won't see Eurydice again,
Ophelia won't start swimming,
and our assassinated Presidents
won't resume their leadership.
I'm sick of Dunkin' Donuts bags,
of plastic pints of vodka,
chocolate milk gone sickly,
Milky Way wrappers flapping
on the rim of the marsh where peepers
chant in a disciplined chorus.
I bag the trash so emphatically
it squeals in protest. Old friends
would laugh at my flailing gestures,
but they've all died and left me
to patrol the boundary between
nature and culture by myself.
The sun has gained some strength

and I sweat enough to attract
a maze of blackflies keening
their indelible, inaudible rage.
My bag is full. I heft it home
to deliver to the landfill,
where even the feisty dreams fade,
leaving only the faintest
and least offensive odors.

The Paleontology Convention

Once I had scattered my ashes
I thought I was done with myself.
Yet I found myself whole again,
and walked to the convention center
where ogling paleontologists
told me you'd gone for coffee
with a finely textured gentleman.
The entire city felt aroused.
Storefronts glittered like glaciers.
In a steamy café Larry hailed me
with a lanky skein of gossip.
Not about you but our colleague
who like me had died of shame.
Larry was pleased I'd resurrected,
if just for secular reasons,
but wondered why my office mate
refused to refute his demise
in similar terms when everyone
had forgotten or forgiven words
lavished in wasteful colors.
"No one had listened anyway,"
Larry confided through his beard.
He left to meet a woman shaped
like a nineteen-fifties jukebox.
Then you gestured at the window,
having satisfied your lover
by smacking him with a textbook
heavy with that coated paper
stinking of multiple-choice exams.

You were almost glad I'd risen
from my remains, but groused
that my red tie clashed with my shirt.
"That's not a tie but an open wound,"
I responded. You tasted the blood
and pronounced it cheap Merlot.
Maybe the next time I recurred
I would nurse on a richer vintage
and leave the fossil-self behind.

Dracula in Peterborough

Downtown on Sunday morning at the only bakery open, we join a little mob slobbering over treats. The dim light in the bakery illuminates a hunger that infects everyone the way the current virus does: by word of mouth. We pay for our snacks and retreat to the riverside, where benches offer lumbar support. Savoring our brown-bagged baked goods and coffee, we feel adventurous, and look forward to a day of gardening and reading dull old books. A figure drifts toward us. It's the embodiment of hunger we had hardly noticed in the corner. It's Count Dracula, his fangs exquisite with scrimshaw, his silver-tipped cane probing the pebbled walkway. Do we speak Romanian? Yes, of course we do. He looks as friendly as a puppy. He sits down to chat a while. What do people do in this punky little town? he wants to know. We read, ogle the young, commit silly little crimes, crash our cars into each other. What else does one do in a culture without culture? The Count nods, looking wise. The sunlight on the silver tip of his cane looks bold as a hole through one's head. You whisper, "I thought sunlight killed vampires," but the Count looks healthy and strong, his self-satisfaction warming us as well. We examine the baked goods we've purchased. I break off a chunk of scone while you bite into a blueberry muffin. The count nibbles a Napoleon fresh from the oven. He licks the cream from his lips and murmurs, "To hell with that blood diet." We all sip our coffee. We're bulking up, becoming a nation of carbohydrates. The sugar high is ineluctable.

Extinct Creatures Are Stalking Us

Dinosaur tracks in the yard
this morning. Shallow but large
Eons sometimes overlap,
arousing bedrock with new ideas
and challenging evolution
in terms science can't define.

You worry that massive heaps
of dinosaur dung will crush
gentian and other late bloomers;
but aside from a cornflower
crushed by a clumsy paw, I find
no damage worth reporting
to the fish and game department,
which handles dinosaur sightings.

The day blooms as August days do,
winsome with a hint of thunder.
The news includes a photograph
of the President rallying right-
wing citizens, and another
of a crashed airplane burning.
Everyone survived that wreck,
but will retain the sensation
of worlds dropping away from them
for the rest of their unnatural livres.

You rake away the dinosaur tracks
before I can photograph them

and send the images to experts
who can identify the species.
Wouldn't you like to know which
extinct creatures are stalking us?
I'll brew coffee and toast some toast
and we can discuss over breakfast
which lost age is our favorite.

The cloudy light pours over you
as you work. For a moment
you look pre-Darwinian
as if draped in colors the earth
hasn't seen since the asteroid strike
sixty-six million years ago,
the moment we were born.

The Romance of Old Clothes

Whether I'm wearing it or not,
my old green sweater regards me
with a sneer of ancestral disdain.

This is why I prefer old clothes:
their attitude. You worry
that holes in my winter garments

chill parts of me no one,
including me, has ever seen.
Spongy old shoes whimper

as I slop along Grove Street.
My trousers sag and bag and sigh.
The rich old women shopping

for cheap trinkets for grandkids
avoid my nearsighted gaze,
shunning my apparent need.

You urge me to clear my closet
of masses of flannel rags
and buy a shiny new outfit

and present myself freshly minted.
But the guck of thaw underfoot
would molt the shine from new shoes,

and the splat of run-over puddles
would render cheerful trousers moot.
Let's wait until spring to discuss

my wardrobe and its discontents.
My green sweater almost loves me,
and my checked gray flannel shirt

clings to me with desperation.
The holes in my blue jeans earn me
a dollop of teenage envy,

and my fuzzy old watch cap
perks on my head like a pet.
Even you admit that my black parka

doesn't look all that rusty.
And when the snow gets deep enough,
my tall rubber boots, sole-worn,

cradle my feet with gentle care.
No, real poverty lurks elsewhere,
cowering in the flux of weather.

Lacking adequate fuel and food,
certain local households suffer
cries of badly crumpled infants,

and can't solve the difficult math
of vast international wealth.
My old green sweater understands.

And so do my thick old socks, despite
the holes in their heels through which
I feel so much cruelty plotting.

From the Tree Alphabet

A lone word stuck in the fork
of a white oak deep in the woods.
light flickering through it
to expose its intricate structure
like something angelic and true.

I can't read it from here. Too old
and brittle to climb the tree,
I peer into the shudder and gloss
of wind-teased canopy and catch
the blush of a single letter
from that infamous tree alphabet
only deceased savants can read.

But I want to know who placed
that word in the tree and why
it clings there against the wind.
I want to know if it's scrawled
on paper or on seamless air.
Mixed motions propel the woods
from one moment to the next.

Age is not an issue for trees
as long as their roots can touch
something essential in the soil.
I lack the sap to anchor me
so firmly to the living process,
which I'm sure that one word explains.

Maybe I should attempt the climb
despite my stiff and aching legs,
my awkward L-shaped arms
that once were athletic enough
to hoist me into atmospheres
not everyone could enjoy.

I watch the word flutter like
a pennant and want to cheer,
but it might condemn me if
I misread it, or maybe even
if I read it and understood.

Garden Grief

Already deer have pruned hosta
from which I had expected leaves
large enough to shade the world.

This will be a summer of sighs
and hurricanes, the Atlantic
coughing up the thickest vapors,

the Leeward Islands cringing.
These hosta would have spoken
a windy floral language

almost audible to people like me
willing to sit all day and listen.
Thunder will mock the absence

of those flapping leaves. Also
the lack of birdsong will goad
harsh winds from the east where

beaches erode to reveal the wreck
that once was civilization
before the great shame struck.

I shouldn't be so troubled by
the vegetarian greed of deer.
I spray repellent on the many

surviving hosta, hoping their leaves
grow large enough to shield me
from my foolish little fears.

The chewed stumps regard me
with reproach. Why hadn't I sprayed
this stinking repellent earlier?

A typical spring grimace
overlays this scene. I kneel
in the dirt and study its texture.

Everyone knows it's really flesh,
but only under the greatest stress
are we willing to admit it.

The Dream of the Toads

Although it's midwinter, the dream
of the toads sings through the chill,

seething and simmering and filling
the day, conjuring riper seasons.

Walking by the half-frozen marsh,
I let that dream enhance me

with those primal russet passions
Thoreau enjoyed but resisted

in light of the Enlightenment.
The collective dream smokes from

holes where those creatures hibernate.
It congeals and becomes audible

like the flight of an arrow
the instant before it strikes you.

Thoreau thought all nature spoke
through this dream. But no one else

seemed to hear it. I wouldn't,
either, if I weren't walking alone

with my head empty as a shell
on a beach. The toads don't care

who overhears or shares their dream.
The tattered look of January

after a couple of days of thaw
conducts the electric shudder

of the dream of the toads as surely
as a glance conducts illicit desire.

I'm tempted to slog across the marsh
and approach the source, but the ground

looks mucky enough to absorb me;
and the ice on the shallows, despite

a glint of sun, looks sad and gray.
The dream of toads keeps fluttering

inside me. But when I get home
it dissipates like a vision

of a richly upholstered future,
divinely sparked, soon forgotten.

Incest of the Arts

You say that the orange and yellow forest resounds like Schubert. I say it tinkles like Bartok, or swings like Glen Miller. You're angry that I take your metaphor-making so lightly. Maybe I'm too old to appreciate the incest of the arts. Maybe I'm too candid to deserve your sunrise smile. The day is passing like a kidney stone. You drive with determined focus, hoping to run me over although I'm in the passenger seat beside you. Look—a hieroglyphic of geese scratched in the slate of sky. Don't try to count them as you drive. I'll tell you if they have as many movements as a Schubert quartet or as Bartok's Concerto for Orchestra. That has five movements, none of them as solemn as you are. Schubert's Death and the Maiden, String Quartet Number Fourteen, has four movements. But there are at least a dozen geese in that shaky vee overhead. No, don't look—you'll run over that man walking his dog. He has named the dog Franz, or maybe Béla. Regardless, the dog is looking up at the geese and barking his little head off, lancing with sharp sounds the fragile autumn light.

Not Art but Apery

Because you hate photography,
which is "not art but apery,"
you've buried my camera in dunes
behind your house on the Cape.
You claim that only the mind
can process imagery precisely
in the four dimensions required.
Only the human brain can render
multi-point perspective
in spiritual geometry rich
enough to please the connoisseur
who flourishes in each of us.
Sea wind sculpts the dunes in shapes
too subtle to parse at a glance.
The sea itself rumples in colors
I can't say are blue, green, or gray
and can't affix in memory.
You with your accented speech,
your distant tinge of Russia,
insist I sketch on good rag paper
my post-impression of a lifetime
spent admiring surf and haze.
The pencil droops in my hand.
The damp air curls the paper.
You dare me to test the eye
against the curls and slope of dunes.
I fail so badly that I draw
someone's naked torso, surely
not yours, slumping in a tub

of brackish yellow water: more
a crime scene than an artwork.
But maybe when you taunt me
with rants against technology
this is exactly what you mean.

The Architecture of Hauntings

Upper floors are always haunted. The attic of my family home wheezes with spirits two hundred years past. Greasy apparitions smut the two small second-floor bedrooms in Tara's house. The Breakers' grand stairway of marble and gilt can't tempt me to ascend to the creepy servants' rooms high above the ground-floor library, dining room, and ballroom. The crooked wooden chimney-winding staircase in the House of Seven Gables forbids me from confronting the dead whispering to each other beneath a complex joinery of roof. Even the loft of your expensive condo sports the ghost of a long-departed lover, whose checked twill jacket flaps like a sail in the gloom. I'm safer living on one floor. Yes, I'm happy with bedroom, bath, and kitchen all at ground level so if the ghosts arrive I can escape through any window. Maybe the basement bears a spook or two, but I only do my laundry there. The grumble of the washer and whirr of dryer warn off the worst manifestations: those you in your grimmer spiritual moments persuade yourself to endorse.

Your Infinity Suit

Wearing your infinity suit,
you're invisible to everyone
but me. The shimmer of its surface
clings to you like plastic wrap,
while absence of color conceals you
and doesn't even cast a shadow.

Dressed in this impossible distance,
you prowl the streets and observe
lovemaking in the gutters,
homeless people kneeling in prayer,
thick men dying in the doorways
of houses abandoned decades ago.

You enter rich apartment blocks
and slip into upholstered rooms
and fondle delicate knickknacks
and flip through famous first editions
and sample elaborate dinners
and sip wines you could never afford.

You listen to couples debate
sending their children to prep schools
or investing in blue-chip stocks,
then yawn so loudly with boredom
they startle and look all around
at the apparently empty air.

I can see you while others can't,
but that's because I carry
a mental photograph of you naked
not as people commonly are,
but as raw marble looks naked
to the eye of the expert sculptor.

Yes, the gleam of the suit itself
lingers for a moment not
where you are but where you were
a moment ago. I follow you
down the avenue, the crowd
parting in the shock of your breath.

Maybe if I ask politely
with that humble look on my face
you'll let me try on that suit
on some warm dull afternoon when
infinity seems a reckoning
worth a little bodily risk.

Penny Postage

Old postcards of antique ruins
or landmarks since demolished
by twentieth-century wars
comfort me on winter nights
when the moon casts milky shadows
and coyotes rasp far away.

Dresden before the firestorm.
Coventry's Gothic cathedral.
The Sphynx faceless and brooding.
Great Buddhas Taliban destroyed.
The Cloth Hall in Ypres before
German artillery leveled it.

You gave me these to remind me
of Walter Benjamin and Derrida.
You hope that on my birthday
I'll appreciate outliving
the snail-mail picture postcard
still offered on rotating metal racks
but ignored by smartphone tourists.

Shuffling these postcards of losses
and rubble, I deal them out
like the Tarot pack. No hanging man,
but a photograph of catacombs
outside Rome, and one of dusty men
swinging shrunken heads by the hair.

You insist my fortune lies untold
in this array of vanished glories.
Yet some of these places still exist—
the pyramids still gloating with pride,
the tower of Pisa still leaning,
the Colosseum still colossal
although dropping a stone or two.

These postcards render everything
older than the planet itself—
the atonal black and white photos
or stippled machine-made color,
the simple captions, the schoolish
penmanship of the sender.

Everyone who mailed these postcards
died long ago, but these clues
linger like crumbs after meals
eaten when all remembered how
to handle their knife, spoon, and fork.

Blizzard in Pandemic

Bracing for heavy wet snow
that will topple beloved trees
and strangle the electric lines,

I try to maintain my personal
geometry by sitting upright
like a demigod on a throne.

You're more active, snugging cats
in their bolster beds, placing
flashlights to find in the dark.

Even at dawn the thickening
of everything outdoors feels
like a layer of wet felt applied

by a huge demented milliner.
We've been through this before—
days without power, the dark

critiquing the usual Christmas.
If we survive to plow the snow
from the driveway and descend

to the post-storm village, we'll find
the pandemic still in charge,
masks required despite the tears

of frustration streaking our faces.
We need milk, butter, and eggs,
but who can trust the fridge

on such an uncertain morning?
Better stay home and recount
the dream lives that embarrass

without physically harming us.
We can lose ourselves in each
other's collage, plying image

upon image the way the snow
will, revising every surface
until the falsehood is complete.

Morning Melody

The light breaks into pieces small
enough to swallow. This happens
daily, but who notices? Lines
of force stretch like kite strings.
You expect me to do something
with my hands, but arthritis
has rendered them crude as paddles.

Let's go downtown and drown
our quarrels in large paper cups
of high-acid java brewed
to flush sinkers fried in deep
fat fryers no one ever cleans.
Fueled by this gastric adventure,
we'll face a full day of errands
and shuck the scholarly ambitions
that aroused us in our youth.

What good did all that scribbling
on notecards do? Remember
the abstractions of Derrida,
Bachelard, Empson, Hegel?
We dragged their books to the landfill
years ago, purging our senses.

Now we live on the ignorant edge
where the wind brawls from the south.
Our angle of vision excludes
the darker sides of planets

that dangle in the night sky
like demented Christmas ornaments.

No wonder the light seems fractured
along those emphatic lines of force.
Morning coffee usually comforts
and heals the worst of our sins.
But today the news is so bad
the headlines kill even casual
readers with stark efficiency.

Maybe we'll stay home and listen
for mice in the walls. Come outside
and examine the world. The wreckage
of last night's freight of dreams lies
rusting in the garden where
we're likely to trip over it,
sprawling on our Mother Earth.

Reeking of the Equinox

The sour breath of trash cans
overflows into the park.
The rain has depleted our moods.

Still masked against contagion,
people loom at each other and shout
their differences, promising war.

We can't eat this anger although
it barbecues the air between us.
The riverbank buckles and coughs up

mud from the bottom of its heart.
If we could be so generous
we could resettle our politics

in a fresh landscape brimming
with proto-Scandinavian neat.
But the buzz-saw of rhetoric

with cartoonish fervor hacks
a ditch a mile deep to sever
this neighborhood from that one,

where garden gnomes have revolted
and taken the taxpayers hostage.
We should rescue them from looming

abuse of their meager paychecks,
but they would sneer and fail to thank us.
How did we get so disparate?

Something evil in the trash cans
refuses to die. Something reeking
of the equinox, objecting

to the early arrival of dark.
We can't read each other's mask
but suspect a broad complicity.

The river stumbles along, sad gray
and teary. Too cold to wade,
too wide even for children to leap.

The stink of uncollected trash
represents debris trapped in us,
making us too heavy to float.

Dreams of Beautiful Cities

Street patterns I dreamt last night
wouldn't fit into Paris, Rome,
Shanghai, Delhi, or Cape Town.
You would need a clean white plat
to map them, and several bald spots
on the planet to accommodate
the earthwork to render them real.

We all dream of beautiful cities,
starlit palaces and neon dives
where couples exchange genetics
without the faintest hint of shame.
Railroads bundled like wiring,
marble facades unscarred by mold.
Housing of antiseptic plastics
from chemical plants that never
pollute or burst into flames.

You often report such cities
erupting like fungus in places
no one would ever look for them.
You dwell on and in their villas,
townhouses, luxury apartments—
the upper levels of construction.
But I dream of the layout, plumbing,
the underground cables, the poured
concrete vaults of the subways.

I dream at this level because
I wanted to be a city planner
until I realized that cities
refuse to be planned. Lagos, London,
Cairo, New York. They grow
from seed and sprawl. China
believes its new cities are planned,
but they'll run riot, grow weedy
and rank as cities and people do.

Our lifelines are shorter now
than the avenues I mapped last night.
Still, we can walk the length of them
from downtown to wooded suburbs
and explore the quieter side streets
and learn how the built world smothers
the natural one, beginning
with the dross inside our heads.

The Scent of August

The scent of August disperses
in a shatter of spent blossoms.

You probe the earth for excuses
and find nothing to write down

in your book of common failures.
More hurricanes are brewing

in the mid-Atlantic where flocks
of long-flight seabirds reckon

latitude by instinct and faith.
I watch you wield your garden tools,

rake, shovel and hoe, and wonder
if you believe that the autumn

with its cruel election season,
will resolve your ancestral fears.

We both hope for salvation
of the earthly kind, the wobble

of the axis tilting our way.
We expect the solar system

to retain its lilt and harmony
despite certain local effects.

The deluge may be plotting
in certain angles and planes,

but we expect it to save us
by watering our garden

so firmly we'll never have to
soak it with unwanted tears.

Esthétique des Odeurs

The dog has smelled everything,
but not this. He recoils and plops
droopy on the sidewalk, nonplussed.
You laugh at his muddled expression,
but something in terminal decay,
if that's what he thinks he's sensing,
troubles instinct and evolution.

Dogs are entitled to meditate
on any odor they choose,
usually preferring the fetid—
but this defies meditation.
You wonder if some political
object passed, rubbing its thighs
on the fence, leaving a spoor
to attract the opposite sex.

"What sex is the opposite
of politics," I ask. You sigh,
"the absence of sex and also
the afterglow of fantasy sex."
The smell must be powerful enough
to smelt all smells into one.
The dog no longer works his nose—

some knowledge is best left unknown.
Dogs admire the fragrance of death,
rolling in carcasses to hide
their own smell from enemies.

Color-blind, they find color
in the fourth dimension where scent
becomes bravura of rhetoric.

You wish you could nose out crimes
among our little coterie
of town officials, lawyers, cops.
I agree that the local riffraff
offers a world of rotten objects
we trod upon daily, soiling
our shoes but offering subjects
and verbs we can manipulate.

Despite what our favorite poet claims,
evil lacks an aesthetic other
than a range of bouquets a French
parfumier would love to catch.
The dog smelled something stronger,
richer and more frightening
than the usual bundle of sins.

You examine the fence. Nothing
but a slight gray stain as if
some aged person had shed
a year or two in passing. I kneel
in the grass and touch the spot.
I can't smell it, but its texture
is rough as the tongue of a cat.

The dog growls. He objects to
further inquiry. The sun occludes
itself, tucked into cloud. You bark
a warning, but the moment passes,

and you and I and the dog look
ashamed for fussing over
some lunatic notion long past.

Riding the Comet

Two power cars and a coach—
a machined aluminum tube
varnished against corrosion.

Riding the *Comet* from Boston
to Providence unsettles me
since this is a ghost train scrapped

when I was only five years old.
A few dry skeletons crumpled
in faded upholstery smelling

of mold and last century's mice.
As the only living passenger
I huddle in the rear in case

this flimsy speedster crashes.
But ghost trains almost never crash.
And they rarely stop at stations

like Back Bay, which flashes past
in symmetries of concrete platforms.
Then underground to Forest Hills,

slinking along to Readville,
then raging over the marshland,
the Neponset River a flash

of gray. Then past Norfolk without
a pang of conscience. Canton, Sharon,
Foxboro and other suburbs

hardly crease my mental map.
We rip across the state line
and pierce a hole through Pawtucket.

At last I detrain from the dream
with Rhode Island's snowy tombstone
of a state house hovering nearby.

Panting smuts of diesel exhaust,
the *Comet* departs in the mist.
I join myself in a café where

I describe my railroad journey
with respect for the disbelief
self and other have in common.

Did that ghost train actually run?
That gleam of aluminum banded
with two shades of blue enamel

could be enjoyed as winter light
refreshed and refreshing itself
in a corner of our mutual eye.

Rules of Perspective

If we could fold the Amazon
rain forest into a packet
and hide it in a safe place,
we would. If we could decorate
every nook with orioles, wrens,
and wood and hermit thrush, we would.

Autumn stumbles into view,
one orange maple after another.
Serial notions of defeat
may warp the horizons beyond
recognition, displacing senses
we've trusted for many years.

Let's prepare ourselves by learning
Leonardo's rules of perspective
and applying them to each other.
The cats that die of cancer,
the children who die of boredom,
the horses toppled in the field
testify that entropy applies
to even our favorite scents.

The first whispers of wood smoke
loft above the village. Teenage
criminals prowl with vapid sneers.
If we could educate their hormones
to apply only when needed,

we would. A federal judge just ruled
that silence implies guilt. But here,

by a river exploited by drought,
we lie in the grass and enjoy
the hush of a smoke-yellow sky
blown all the way from the west coast
where wildfires assert themselves
in a mixture of colors not even
Leonardo could hope to apply.

An Art Deco Version of the Panama Canal

Your neighborhood grew hilly
in my absence, the houses
clinging to unruly slopes.

You redecorated to suggest
an Art Deco version
of the Panama Canal but

that drippy neighbor squatting
at your dining room table quotes
Coleridge and George Herbert to prove

how culturally advantaged she is.
I should have stayed home but
wanted to watched the workers

resurrecting the old railroad
that before the latest earthquake
trundled through your back yard

with container-loads from China.
Piecing together their language
of grunts and groans I learn that

a coppery autumn discontent
has settled over this city,
wrenching men from needed sleep

and drying up the mother's milk
that fuels your future leaders.
After resetting and polishing

miles of rail, the workers burn
their favorite tools with ritual
prayers to invoke the moon.

In response it rises, a full moon
veiled by pumpkin-colored mist.
You've said nothing about the cries

of blackbirds parsing funerals,
of delinquents breaking into
storage sheds where militias

store their nuclear weapons.
You neighbor quotes her last quotation
and gusts through the back door

with a gesture of sweeping disdain.
I claim the chair she warmed,
and pretend to admire the carpet

you laid, Panama gray
with a fringe of jungle. Your smile
is ravenous. The day declines

toward a stainless climax no one
who hasn't savored your small talk
can fully perceive or admire.

Pattern is Purpose

Watching Canada geese paddle
across the fly pond convinces me
that pattern is purpose. Why else
would the ripple of their wake

mime the wind-response of pines
and the shiver of naked lovers?
On this lithographed afternoon
the geese are unafraid of me,

but prefer the far shore where
there's no bench to seat me
for a Zen moment or two.
No reckless lovers, either,

although one drab evening I glimpsed
sleek bodies parsing each other
while trout bubbled up for mayflies.
The mind settles easily here—

the pond almost perfectly round,
the plantation of red pines planted
in strict ranks, the geese half-tame.
Centered in weight I distribute

through my carefully seated self,
I try to honor distinctions
among the non-human elements—
the geese, the water, the texture

although not the stance of the pines.
Only another human presence
could further refine this scenery.
But I always come here alone

to avoid startling even simple
life forms like trout and insects
and in winter the snow-ghosts
that glide so gently over the eye.

The Household God Died

The enameled winter light
perfects itself without regard
for the weeping in the kitchen,
the suicide in the attic,
the child hiding in the crawl space
between this dimension and that.

I remember the very moment
that the household god died
of dust, boredom, and neglect.
Even on a bright afternoon,
dark congealed in the corners
of every room. My mother
looked up from her book to greet
something from her own childhood,
while next door my grandfather
sighed his last tobacco sigh
and consigned himself to vapor.

At the funeral my father shook
his fist at the Catholic ghost
smoking from the big brass censer.
He already knew that the priest
had an evil way with children.
He had sent me to the other church,
where no superstition burdened
the sleek rectors of disbelief.

Now the season has parsed itself
down to the final dismay.
Filthy roadside snow heaps
fester. Last year's ambitions
collapse as the stock market falls
in fear of virus from China.

After many years, the household
god has yet to resurrect.
I hesitate to assign a gender
to a gust of chill, a shadow,
but if he should return, he'll find
the same world of freeze and thaw
confusing form with content.

The Trees Think in Solemn Tones

Even in winter drab the trees
think in solemn tones from which
we infer disaster's coming.
The die-off of insects occurring
beneath our vision and skins
will sever the food chain and leave
cartoon exclamation points
etched in the sky overhead.

Not even your three sad years
fending off bullies and thugs
in the Girl Scouts can atone
sufficiently for the viscous
sound of souls abandoning
their exoskeletons to enter
space much broader and deeper
than our imaginations allow.

The trees consider the problem
from various elevations,
waving their wind-happy boughs,
and agree upon a solution.
If photosynthesis should cease
for one year we would smother
in our stony beds and relinquish
the scripture that dooms everything.

I hear this conspiracy texting
from one tree to another in

sobs of gray wind. But you doubt
that the trees are so organized,
and believe that like us they'd spurn
to share among different species:
ash disdainful of pine, maple
distrusting hemlocks and birch.

The die-off is real, though; only
the nastiest tree-killers likely
to survive: gypsy moth, ash
borer, Asian longhorn beetles
wooly adelgids, bark beetles, aphids.
Having survived the Girl Scouts,
shedding that scratchy uniform,
you aren't afraid of these creatures.

But late at night when the chewing
and boring becomes audible
in the dark of the inner ear
I worry that the planet
isn't dying solemnly enough—
its suffering too personal
to scrawl in clumsy longhand
and nail to the tallest pine.

Black Dog, White Dog / White Dog, Black Dog

A black dog and a white dog,
happy mixed-breed littermates.
Shampooing at the groomer's
washes off the dye their owner
applied merely to amuse us.
The black dog becomes white,
the white dog becomes black.
Their tails still wag in the same
direction, their joy unabated.

We laugh off this omen,
a harmless prank, but the news
is bad: storms are shouldering
over the mountains to the west,
murders spike in Chicago
and New York, right-wing senators
rant and foam at the mouth,
the army is on full alert
with unnamed enemies massing
along the Canadian border.

The dogs don't notice that one
was white and is now black,
the other black and now white.
Despite being freshly bathed,
they want to play in the mud
by the river, where last year
the corpse of a child washed up.

No one claimed her, no one
had reported her missing, no one
fainted at the sight of her face.

We observe the dogs rolling
by the river, then splashing
into the iron current, their smiles
infectious and indiscriminate.
We sip our coffee and discuss
the latest political dramas.
After a while the two dogs
approach us for pets and praise
and to shake half a river's worth
of fish-stink all over us,
completing the morning critique.

The Dogs Have Learned to Talk

All the dogs have learned to talk.
They're discussing the rising cost
and poor ingredients of pet food.
They won't speak to their owners,
but when I ask a passing boxer
his name he replies, "Aloysius."

You're undisturbed by this glib
new phenomenon. Perched
on a metal chair on the lawn
before the bookstore, you indulge
your bitter appetite, preferring
a lumpy scone to conversation.

Do you think that public discourse
has gone to the dogs? October
is almost here, your favorite month.
I had hoped we would hike in hills
of seasonal flamboyance, shedding
the bulge of a summer of leisure.

I had hoped that some great logic
would empower us when alone
with vees of geese honking overhead.
The dogs talk so loudly no one
merely human can interrupt.
Although leashed to their masters,

the dogs have seized control without
a hint of violence. Their diction

is perfect, their sense of the *bon mot*
enviable. Finish your scone
and allow me a sip of your coffee.
I hope that when we get home

our cats remain as wordless
and private as always. I wish
I could emulate their stance
despite the oceans of language
heaving between us, between us
and whatever's about to evolve.

A Letter to Hart Crane

Dear Hart: two saltwater-sodden
bundles of newsprint arrived
today, all that remains of you
after your interrupted voyage.
I scan the headlines: MAN -EATING
SHARK exclaims one front page; SHARK-
EATING MAN reads the other.

Whoever sent me these bundles
expects me to make a papier
mâché mannequin of you
from this briny muddle of news
from the Twenties when you roamed
waterfront bars with Emile,
the love of your lovelorn life.

No one in this grizzled town
reads poetry except pale women
recently smitten with Robert Frost.
The mannequin will represent you
as Walker Evans portrayed you—
serious, almost sober enough
to challenge small-town rhetoric.

You can shout everyone down
by working consonants so hard
they crack underfoot like snails.
You can describe your drowning
in the most vulgar terms and earn

the pity of men who served in wars
and had lonely sex in foxholes.

Not that a sculpted paste statue
is likely to speak loudly enough
for everyone to appreciate.
But you and I will converse
in sundown colors too subtle
to impress anyone who hasn't
lived a long time under the sea.

Blue Mammoth Hosta

Last night I heard a long ripping sound but didn't realize that a plant was uprooting, preparing to relocate. At dawn I saw my blue mammoth creep across the yard with huge paddle-leaves working the air. I ran out to grab it and return it to its plot, but it shrugged me off with ease. I hadn't realized hostas could get so hostile, that they could be so strong. It's big, a good six feet across, but I'm big, too, and have good hands. Not good enough, though. The blue mammoth sidles up to the house and splats against it. It's crushing a clutch of day lilies, but I guess that's something plants must settle among themselves. Now in the scalding heat of noon I see that the critter has moved along, down to the far, shady end of my property. It seems to be looking out at the view of Monadnock. I'm tired of wrestling with this thing. It's been uprooted so long it's probably weakening. I's only a plant isn't it? I I grab a leaf and tug, and after a token struggle it consents to follow me back to the garden. To coax it back into the ground, I've renovated the location from which it uprooted. I've lined the hole with fresh loam and a dose of plant food. The hosta looks suspicious, but circles like a dog about to lie down. At last it settles in place, and I tuck the soil around its roots. I'd swear that it's smirking, but I don't see how it can do that without a mouth.

Arcadia in Plague

To conceal the latest dread,
we mask ourselves in public.
It doesn't help. Churches tilt
away from us, storefronts blind
their facades with heavy plywood,
our close friends estrange themselves
behind faces crude as ours.

Ben Jonson thought that masques
rendered allegories thick enough
to spoon-feed finicky royalty.
His characters didn't express
but relied on song and gesture
to convey their metaphysics.

We don't sing because cloth stifles
even the wispiest whispers.
We don't gesture large gestures
because we learned from Chaplin
how insistent mime can seem.

The streets fold in on themselves
like old-fashioned aerograms.
Men climb out of pickup trucks
with their covered faces sweating.
Maybe we're all ripening toward
some fecund but final harvest.

We enter the only grocery store
that still stocks living fruit.
Oranges, lemons, a cantaloupe.
What if these are shrunken heads
of those who've died of boredom,
waiting for the plague to catch up?

We fill our baskets and pretend
the sky pressing at the window
is merely friendly and curious.
The whole checkout line shudders
like a runover snake. The great
collective masque absorbs us
into settings so anonymous
no one bothers forwarding mail.

Ringing Difficult Changes

Do you hear a constant tingling
in your mind? Metal on metal,
it seeps from the recycling center
and lodges in the human genome,
where every hint is fodder.

The village clenches in misery
as, one by one, shops close forever,
unlocked doors banging in the wind,
unsellable goods abandoned,
tainted by criminal proteins.

We should stay home with doors
and windows sealed against smells
discolored by strong ultraviolet.
We should read those dreary books
we've been putting off for decades.

I think someone in a monk's robe
is ringing difficult changes
with a fervor dredged from the past.
Don't listen, don't try to understand—
the old bronze speaks in tongues.

We can't waste any more time
in our favorite café because
it went out of business, leaving
scorch marks on an old pine floor.
We can't expect the post office

to deliver us from evil.
The hardware store, source of many
unkempt noises, still accepts cash
or check, the elderly clerks
grinning like Jolly Roger.

Ignore any sound that suggests
we've passed into a digital gloom.
A lone crocus erupts in the yard.
Consider it the equivalent
of the last impromptu kiss.

Winter Approaches Harrisville

Old brick mill buildings nosing
forward into December,
eager for the new year when
small frozen rivers resolve
and citizens like us repent.

With most of a century wasted
on the human project (the curve
of the earth flattened, the point
of vanishing point perspective lost),
I lean against a cold northerly,

unable to distinguish post-
Canadian gray from local
shades, the ice rim of the lake
sharper than a guillotine.
Whoever devised such cruelty

should languish on the bottom
long enough to cringe as tightly
as a rosebud plucked too soon.
You say it's only nature
applied with strokes of an old

fashioned Speedball pen, the kind
cartoonists used last century
when we still retained our humors.
You remind me that when the lake
has sealed itself we can cross it

and count the drowned faces peering
up through the optical ice.
Do you recall how many we saw
last year? The year before? The mills
used to grind people small enough

to stop caring that their hands hurt.
The low pay guaranteed misery
so thickly upholstered in snow
that no one noticed the neighbors
had also lost fingers or limbs.

This year we should walk the ice
after dark, see if the faces glow
with the phosphorescence of decay.
Maybe this time we'll remember
how many, what they have to say.

Wanton Weather

Snowfall wears a surgical mask
in this age of feckless disease.

Because it clings to every surface,
it risks spreading a virus

powerful enough to French-kiss
every virgin into a frenzy.

I'm afraid to go out and shovel
the spongy mess from the driveway.

Already I can taste its lewd
and acidic texture laving

over my face as I strain to lift
shovelful after shovelful

to only the faintest applause.
Let's stay indoors and watch it melt.

But you with your germproof snowsuit
have already rushed into the storm.

Before I get my boots laced up
you've cleared a path to the road

so the Mask of Red Death can find us,
if he happens to be on the prowl.

The daylight's too thick to swallow
without difficulty. The roar

of oil burner in the basement
reassures with the ancient language

of fire brought smartly up to date.
What would Faustus say if faced

with this slur of wanton weather?
Would he feel his soul collect itself,

don a parka, and set out to meet
the devil at the bend in the road?

I feel nothing but the snowfall
plastering every detail

to render the landscape rococo
and mock our aesthetic mood.

The Monster of Myself

Being the monster of myself
both comforts and frightens me.
I tried to shock the crowds back
to low-lying places littered
with the bones of hurricanes,
the rags of historic moments.

Last night I raged into a room
where you had veiled in memory
of the massive husband who flew
to Crete with his final beloved
and crashed into the succulence,
going silent enough to forget.

But you refused to forget,
and draped yourself in a mist.
I pleased myself by rending it.
The monster of me was charmed
by your pale and pink facades while
the human of me wilted in shame.

Paris droops, Siena kneels and weeps,
salt pillars prop up Jerusalem.
The monster has shed a skin,
and claims that a fresh contagion
pours from mountainous districts
to scald the plains ochre and buff.

Anyone could name this monster,
but I must point out that rooms
above shuttered cafes in nations
on the brink of bankruptcy hold
carcasses he's saving for later,
when the cats have muffled their cries.

Being the monster of myself
requires me to do as I please,
rendering simple things naked
but enshrouding people like you
in freshly laundered textiles
where your secrets merge with mine.

The Secret History of Slavery in America

In the blue blush of the wind,
the pines look surly enough
to kill without much conscience.

We must avoid their shadows,
where long-forgotten voices pool.
To avoid perpetuating

this latest and greatest harangue,
we mustn't speak of distance
rooted creations can't achieve.

Today the projected longueurs
will languish like last year's nudes.
Talking heads hysterical over

the latest virus from China
will clog the digital airwaves
and render intellects supine.

Don't mistake all that blather
for the same dull austerity
that claims that wi-fi causes

autism in the vegetable world.
Don't allow yourself to numb
in the clash of competing texts.

Let's discuss this over coffee
the color of privileged flesh.
We agree on political shades

of glory, on the afflatus
of our favorite language-acts.
Let's maintain our regard for

the Founding Fathers although
they fostered the one great sin.
The wind bruises everything

black-and-blue: its insistence
ripe with glamor, yet snooping
into our dearest little shame.

Writing Myself Down a Hole

Dark leaks from wounds in the sky
and puddles in low spots people
like us should avoid. The river
dazzles over bedrock, lighting
the dusk with foam. You expect
to ignite yourself with fireflies,
but their heat hardly registers
on important parts of your skin.

This indecision terminates
every day with equal prejudice,
nailing us to the calendar.
If we could move into town
and barricade indoors with people
lacking surnames, laughing over beer
at the locally famous tavern,
we'd avoid that sense of gasping
for indelible shadows too deep
to belong to anything living.

But we've chosen this absence
and must inhabit it despite
the drag of former urban lives.
The fear is part of our contract
with a silence as drab as granite.
We honor it by trotting home
with nervous candor, leaving tracks
in the road anyone could follow.

The river spits and snarls and weeps
for lost mythologies nothing
can resurrect. To understand
that absence requires great focus
and great fear, more than two people
deprived of lust can muster.

Remind Me What We Believe

Last night, rain bruised so deeply
I arose with handfuls of blood
as if I'd been finger-painting
in every ghastly autumn color.
You want to inspect the basement
for leaks and weeping, but the pumps

stand silent in their sump holes.
You remind me that years ago
I dedicated mornings to writing
the unwritable tale of my life,
but now I waste the smoky dawns
parsing otherworldly topics.

Once I thought I would shape myself
after a famous Cezanne still-life.
But now I resemble a brushstroke
rendered offhand by Franz Kline.
Doesn't matter to the sopping world
adrift at the kitchen window.

Doesn't matter to the cat who died
last week after sitting in my lap
for three hours watching chipmunks
upholster their larders for winter.
I miss his smooth black contours
sculpted to cuddle against me.

The rain was his memorial.
You agree that his little spirit

likely danced the dark rain dance
all night as we lay in the filth
of the Anthropocene, a place
only nonbelievers would love.

Please remind me what we believe
before more rain billows over
places we though we understood—
wooden houses, low rounded hills,
and a tremble of apprehension
when gray lichened boulders crack.

A Damp Spot

A damp spot in the forest.
Mist rises and clots the pine-tops,
erasing distance that enables
my sense of simple geography.

You never worry about your grip
on the planet, and ignore me
when I worry that gravity
will fail on my daily walk
and set me adrift in shades
of gray lacking innuendo.

You rake wet leaves into piles
shaped like extinct animals.
When I help you drag tarp-loads
into the woods I feel funereal.

Bored and exhausted by yard work,
I visit that damp spot and breathe
the mist, absorbing as much of it
as my slack old lungs can swallow.
If I were still a man among men,
I'd lie in that muck and expect
to sink deeply enough to anchor
my body where it belongs.

You'd never bother searching
 for my papery little remains,
but would collect my insurance
and rake away your modest grief.

More rain coming. I'll cover
the firewood I split this morning,
then slip indoors for a sip
of the six-dollar vodka hidden
behind a bag of cat litter,
where it almost never tempts me
to pour it all over myself
and pretend I've gone up in flames.

There Goes All the Ecology

You look forward to Florida
slopping knee-deep in risen sea.
You want it scraped from the map
so its awkward Freudian shape
no longer stirs crude passions.

The Everglades will disappear
in a mush of incongruous tides.
Alligators will pack their bags
and trudge north to conquer Atlanta,
occupying every swimming pool.

Pure glass condominium towers
of Miami Beach will topple
as the sand beneath them ripples
in an undertow more powerful
than the San Francisco earthquake.

You don't want anyone to die
in this rumpling of the elements,
but you want a certain arrogance
to lisp and weep and regret
a racist, land-grabbing history.

But clouds of flamingos scouring
for a fresh environment rebuke
your glee, and the costumes
abandoned by Disney employees
will wash up the coast to beach

only a few miles from your house—
a plastic Mickey Mouse head
left forlorn in tattered seaweed.
Florida is doomed regardless
of your desire to see it drown.

But the angle of your disdain
invites the rising sea to spout
through every bit of plumbing,
rousting innocent homeowners
hoping merely to age in place.

The Anthropocene Has Dawned

Autumn-yellow hosta leaves
slump with terminal dismay.
They didn't travel from Japan
to confront New England winters.
Their disappointment sours
and sticks to the tip of my tongue.

With tiny sighs of reproof,
black spiders escape the woodpile
as I split a whole season of fuel.
The Anthropocene has dawned
in chemical colors no version
of the solar spectrum has parsed.

The gray sound of the absence
of songbirds combs the maples.
You recall a moment of thrush
when the weeds stood upright
and listened with flowering respect.
The light scalded itself almost blind.

You thrilled at three species of frog
rasping around the rim of the marsh.
But with my telescoped vision,
I referred to an avenue creased
by shadows of new skyscrapers
excluding the old horizons.

Toting a bag of groceries, I crossed
against the grain of bus and taxi
and slipped into fresh geometries.
Since then, horizons have relaxed
to accommodate the smelting of ore
undiscovered until this instant—

a broad voice reeking of sulfur
yellow as hosta leaves, stitched
with phonemes richer than sense
can make of them, startling
the maples into dishabille
too graceful for us to attempt.

9 789390 601325